AF350281

Table of Contents

Cybersecurity Jobs

Work from Home

Book 4

Find Cybersecurity Jobs

By

Bruce Brown, CISSP, ISC2 CAP

---

1. *http://www.convocourses.com*

Download free ATS resume templates at:

convocourses.com/courses/resume[2]

Check us out on:

youtube.com/convocourses

Contact us:

contact@convocourses.com

I love working from home!

I have been working from home since 2014, and it's been great!

For me, "working from home" is not about literally working from my house but about having the freedom to work from anywhere.

I have been able to work from the Philippines, Thailand, and Vietnam. South East Asia is one of my favorite places to stay because of the weather, fascinating culture, low cost of living, and good food. Traveling makes me feel a sense of freedom that I don't get from an office.

To be honest, I don't even have to leave the USA to have a good time and feel free. Staycations are also nice. A staycation is where you just go to another city or state and hang out. I have hung out in Las Vegas, Aspen, Vail, Los Angeles, Miami, and other places. I do my regular hours of work, and then, after work, I go check out an art museum with my family, eat at amazing restaurants that are famous with the locals, or just go for a walk downtown.

Before COVID-19, it was harder to get a work from home position. But now, these remote positions are everywhere. During the lockdown, it became a necessity to have remote work capabilities.

As a result, it's now easier than ever to become a remote worker. Some companies have reported seeing an increase in productivity after allowing workers to work from home.

As of 2022, 10% of U.S. employees work from home. According to a study by Stanford Business, where they studied a travel agency with 16,000 employees, working from home saw a 13% increase in performance. Nine percent of this came from working more minutes per shift with fewer breaks and sick days, and 4% from more calls per minute. This increase may have come from a more comfortable and quiet working environment.

Working from home is a win-win scenario. The worker is in the best possible working environment to be more productive.

In this book, I'm going to tell you exactly how to find these remote positions.

Is WFH for you?

The terms WFH, work from home, remote work, telecommute and flex jobs are sometimes used interchangeably in organizations. What is different is how each organization defines them. We will go in greater detail about this, but we need to see if this is even something for you.

First, you should know that working from home is not for everyone. It sounds good, but, believe it or not, some people are not ready for it.

Here are some signs that it's not for you:

- You're an extrovert and absolutely love the feeling of being around many people
- You have small kids and will be disturbed all-day
- You live in a rural area with very poor Internet and electricity
- You struggle with self-discipline
- You don't have access to an Internet connection.
- You're not in an environment where you can work:
    - You don't have a quiet area
    - You don't have a room with privacy

If any of these apply to you and you cannot change the situation, you may want to reconsider the thought of working from home.

A good friend of mine tried doing 100% remote work, and she found out that she did not like it. She said she felt trapped in the house. When she worked remotely, she got depressed and restless.

She actually prefers to go into an office or visit sites to talk to customers and doesn't mind the commute.

I had multiple office coworkers tell me this. One told me he just didn't have the self-discipline to do it, and it was too tempting to sit around and play video games as much as possible. He said he gained a ton of weight and felt terrible. Another coworker told me that he did it for 15 years at IBM and preferred getting out of the house. The office was like a break for him. Remote work is just not for everyone.

Some of the challenges of working remotely

Self-discipline can be a challenge. Not everybody has the self-discipline to wake up in the morning, turn on the computer, and focus entirely on work, especially if there is a beach right outside, the kids want to go for a hike, or the dog wants you to throw the ball. I have to admit sometimes self-discipline is difficult.

Another bad thing about working from home is it sometimes I get close to my coworkers and would like to see them in person.

I've been doing this for many years now, and there are times when I just want to work in a different environment. On rare occasions, I have missed going to an office.

Another challenge of working from home is that sometimes, I get pulled into running errands around the house. These are things that do need to get done but could probably wait until after work.

You can't always do Staycations

I can't always travel when I am working from home. When I have a big project that requires me to lead a bunch of meetings, I am too busy to take the time to travel to a new destination, or I might have to work so many hours that it's not worth going anywhere, and I need to stay in the house.

I usually coordinate my trips so that I am not driving or flying while I am in the middle of my work from home jobs.

I had to do a vulnerability scan at a site, and on my way to the airport, my job kept trying to get a hold of me. Once I parked in long-term parking, I was able to respond to their emails. Every time I am on my way to a staycation spot to work from the Rocky Mountains or near the Las Vegas Strip, there is an emergency that forces me to stop everything I am doing and see what's going on. For this reason, I coordinate any travel time I have for the staycation so that I am en- route to the destination during non-work hours or take a day off unless I am on an actual business trip for my job.

Working after hours

Time management is another challenge you need to master. You would think the issue is working too little, but sometimes it's actually working too much.

One thing we take for granted when working in an office is that it physically separates our personal and work life. One challenge you may have is having the discipline to stop working.

One example from my own life is when I worked as a consultant on a big project and would get so wrapped up in getting it done that I would take calls when I was supposed to be off.

One time, I planned to head to another state with my son. We'd found a Samoyed puppy that we wanted, but the breeder was 700 miles away. Our plan was to head out on Friday right after work at 4:30 pm to Utah.

It had been a long week of reviewing a bunch of security controls for a client. I had already logged out of work when my work phone rang. It was the client.

I was already at a Shell station pumping gas and about to hit the road. I stared at the phone for a moment, debating on whether to answer the phone after business hours.

"Hello, Bruce Brown speaking. May I help you?"

The client had a complaint about the results of the last scan. They said it must have been a false positive because they were certain that they'd cleaned up the vulnerabilities that were showing up.

I assured them I would take a closer look, but the call lasted 10 miles away from the gas station. The client was in such a panic that I decided to call my boss and give him a heads-up. With all of the back and forth, that call cost me another hour of work.

If I had the self-discipline to manage my time, I would have disconnected from work at the end of the duty day.

The moral of the story is do not pick up the call from your job after hours.

The Time Zone Differences

I made it to the Philippines working a 6-figure job! I would be in South East Asia with close friends for a few weeks. We would travel to Thailand and Vietnam to hang out, drink, sightsee, and go to clubs.

But first, I had to finish a few days of work. It was easier said than done because I had to wake up at 10 pm and work until 7:30 am Philippines time. In Colorado, USA (mountain standard time), that was 7:00 am – 4:30 pm. It is a 15-hour time difference.

The hardest part was keeping up with meetings and calls. I had coworkers and clients on Central, Eastern, and Pacific time. Meanwhile, I was trying to keep track of the Philippines' time.

I would use Outlook or Google calendar on Mountain time to keep track. If my coworker said, "Let's have a call at 3 pm," I would make sure to put it on the calendar and send them a meeting invite to confirm the time.

I could not keep the times straight manually. Any attempt to calculate the time zone differences would result in me missing the meeting. So, I used online tools to keep up with time zones and days. I guess some people are very good at this, but I am really bad at keeping track of meetings in different time zones.

I can understand why a person would not want to work remotely. There may come a time when most jobs that can be done remotely will be. It's cheaper for organizations to allow it, making them more resilient against disasters and pandemics.

What You Need to have to Work From Home

Working from home is for people who are self-directed and have the self-discipline to work from anywhere. They can either silence the distractions or find a way to work through them.

- Are you great at managing your own time and don't need a supervisor or boss hovering over your cubicle?
- Are you just as good in meetings on a phone or video call as you are in person?
- Do you feel more comfortable doing work in your home office than in a cold, fluorescent yellow room where people gossip too loud by the water cooler?
- If you have a strong conviction that the time you just spent driving for 25 minutes could have been used to make a cup of coffee and run a vulnerability scan, then you should definitely join Team "Work From Home."

Things You Need Before You Work From Home for Cybersecurity

There are some basic things you will need:

- Stable electricity
- Internet with at least 3 to 12 Megabits per second (4G)
- A room with privacy and quiet
- A computer and a phone
- The right mindset

Electric

Electric power seems too obvious even to mention, but I wanted to talk about it because I have been to some parts of the world that had power spikes, brownouts, and blackouts. For example, when working from provincial parts of Thailand and the Philippines, I had to consider the lack of power. This mostly happens during the rainy season, when there are storms that take out the electricity for hours or even days.

In cybersecurity or any IT type job, I need more than just my phone to work. So, I would have to consider a workaround like a generator, power-saving configurations, additional chargers, or even staying in more expensive parts of the country that are not as impacted by storms.

Electricity is usually not a problem unless I am in a very provincial area of the world, and even then, with proper planning, I am able to keep working.

Internet

The best Internet setup for most work from home jobs is the following:

- Over 3 Megabits per second of stable Internet (download)
- At least 2 Megabits per second (upload)
- (2) separate Internet connections
- Security features enabled on your work laptop and phone
- Private and secure Internet connection
- Wired or Wireless with WPA 2 Encryption
- Access to a VPN (when in public areas)

These days, you can get the Internet just about anywhere because you can use your smartphone as a hotspot. With a decent old 4G connection that gives you a 3 – 12 Megabits per second connection, you can have an Internet connection that's good enough for most jobs.

For most jobs, not all jobs. Depending the amount of video conferencing, streaming, downloads and uploads, you may need way more bandwidth than 3 Megabits. Also, I have found a spotty 3 Megabit per second hotspot to be very problematic, particularly with cybersecurity analyst work where I needed to upload or download 1 Gigabit or larger files.

The rural parts of the USA are a great example where Internet access can be a huge issue. There are areas in Nevada, Colorado, Utah and Wyoming (for example) where it's like a baron wasteland, and there is no cell tower coverage for hundreds of miles. Areas like this would make it impossible to do remote work.

Another thing to consider is having two separate Internet connections. You could have one at home and one from your phone as a hotspot. Or even two phones that allow a hotspot connection. This is helpful because even the best Internet connections goes down from time to time. You want to have a second connection ready.

Security Features on your Computer

Protection of the data on the Internet is also important. With a cybersecurity job, a lot of the information you work with will be sensitive, private, or specialized information that could be damaging if it is made public. As much as possible, you will want to work from a private Internet with at least basic security features like a firewall and antivirus. If you happen to work in a public area, such as the library or Starbucks, you must be mindful of your surroundings and not work on sensitive information. You can use a VPN, a host-based firewall, and host-based intrusion protection, but none of this can guarantee that your system and the data you are working on won't be compromised. For cybersecurity work do not work from a public Internet connection.

If you do use wireless in public or even on your secure home network, you need to use WPA 2 as your encryption. Never use open networks, WEP, or WPA because they are not secure and can easily be hacked.

Storage encryption is another consideration. This will encrypt the data on the work system when it is not being used.

Many of these features will be implemented on a system or mobile device that is provided to you by the employer, but if they don't and you're using your own system, you need to have the following:

- Storage encryption
- Host-based security
- VPNs
- Secure wireless
- Never work from public wireless

You Need a Quiet, Secure Place

You need a place that's both quiet and private because many cybersecurity jobs require regular teleconference meetings where you discuss information or situations that are sensitive.

You may be talking about something within the organization that can hurt their reputation or allow an attacker leverage. For example, suppose you are looking at a bank's vulnerability scan report and you have a meeting with the chief information security officer about which items should be fixed first. In that case, you probably don't want to have members of that bank overhear you talking about it.

Sometimes, it's not just privacy but quiet that you need, just an hour or so of undisturbed silence to get through a meeting or focus on deep analysis of lots of data. This is very difficult to do if you have little kids and cannot lock the doors.

I started this many years ago when my kids were small. They could not understand that their dad had to work. They kept trying to play whenever they saw me.

If you have a separate room where you can separate yourself long enough to do the heavy work, then little kids, loud dogs, or even traffic outside is less of a problem.

Physical security is important to the data you work with. If you cannot secure your work computer or mobile device in a place where it cannot be stolen or tampered with, then working remotely will be a challenge. You need to know that the client's data cannot be accessed or manipulated by unauthorized people. If a person has possession of your work computer, then they can tamper with, corrupt, or steal the data with the right tools.

Other Equipment You May Need

Most of the organizations that had me working from home provided me with a laptop and sometimes a mobile phone. These devices were completely controlled and monitored by the organization. I've been given wireless scanners, thumb drives, and laptop accessories, including a docking station, smart card readers, and an ergonomic desk.

On a few occasions, I had to use my own equipment. I used my own computer and cell phone. These jobs typically did not have sensitive information.

Remote Work Restrictions

One of my favorite things is traveling while doing remote work. But some of the jobs I've worked for have restrictions based on the industry, country, or state laws. For example, as of this writing, the U.S. government has bans on trade with several countries. Some of them are:

- Cuba
- Iran
- Syria
- Venezuela
- China

If you work with the U.S. government handling sensitive information, highly technical equipment, intelligence, national security, or trade secrets, there will be conditions on your travel.

Depending on the job, you may not be allowed to take the organization's equipment outside of the country at all or even work outside of the state. Sometimes these conditions are simply notifying the organization you work for where you're going. You might get a briefing that gives you an idea of the threats in a particular part of the world.

Common travel tips and rules they give you are:

- Maintain physical protection of your government-furnished equipment (GFE) at all times.
- Be suspicious of strangers asking you questions about your job.
- Have situational awareness and always be aware of your surroundings.
- GFE can only be used in approved geographic locations and only for work purposes

The list of barred countries, restrictions, and tips changes from time to time. Before you travel, you will need to get with human resources to read the organization's travel restrictions.

The travel policy will give you a summary of what you can and cannot do without reading through actual federal laws and industry standards.

These policies come from regulations such as Arms Export Control Act (AECA), Export Administration Regulations (EAR), the International Traffic in Arms Regulations (ITAR), and the United States Munitions List (USML). These are United States regulations that restrict and control the export of defense and military-related technologies. This is to safeguard U.S. national security.

And if you're thinking, "Bruce, you're an American asshole! I don't even work for the U.S. government, and I never will! I don't need to think about this stuff at all."

First of all... "Rude."

Second, every country and industry has these types of rules depending on the classification of the information you work with. As a cybersecurity professional, you will have more exposure to sensitive information than in most other career fields.

These regulations include technical data, defense services, aircraft materials, and many other items. The regulations apply to manufacturers, exporters, distributors, 3rd party suppliers, contractors, and software and hardware providers for defense.

To comply with these regulations, organizations register with the State Department or equivalent and adopt an internal policy to enforce the laws. The penalties for violating these regulations are harsh, so they take them seriously.

A friend of mine had a job so sensitive that they (the government or the company or both) controlled and monitored his travel. His job directly affected national security. He had to carry his government phone everywhere he went. It was like a digital leash.

His classification was so high that I asked him if the U.S. government had any information on UFOs and aliens.

And he said...

He said something I would not write in a cybersecurity jobs book.

Most organizations do not have any ITAR restrictions. But if the organization has any affiliation or contract work with the government, there is a good chance that there are international restrictions.

Types of Work from home Cybersecurity Jobs

Many people want to work from home, but if you have never done it before, you should know that not all work from home jobs are equal.

Organizations will have a "remote work," "telecommute," or "work from home" policy where they have rules and restrictions on the remote work that they allow. This makes for a completely different work from home experience at each position.

I have been in different remote work situations, and, honestly, sometimes, it's better to work from the office. Not all remote work is good.

In my experience, you have different types of remote work jobs:

- Flex Work
- Remote with travel
- 100% Remote

Let's talk about each of these.

Flex Work

In cybersecurity, flex work schedules mean you will be expected to work from the office a few times per week. There is usually a reason why these jobs require people to work from the office. Sometimes they require at least weekly face-to-face meetings with the customer.

There are also situations where the data is too sensitive to bring home. In one IT job, I had that was flexible, we had a classified environment that could not be maintained remotely.

We had a lab with a network that had a "Secret" classification. The network had a firewall, routers, switches, and endpoint devices. It could not be accessed remotely. All work on this network was restricted to the lab.

When the commute time is too long, organizations will allow flex work from time to time. I worked at a place that preferred everyone to work from the office, but we were all in different states, so most of your work had to be remote. We had cybersecurity professionals near client sites, but sometimes their commute was over 2 hours, so the organization would allow them to go to the office only when absolutely necessary.

There are some organizations that have a strong culture of comradery and make it mandatory to meet in person a few times a week.

Federal organizations are starting to open up to a flexible work environment to attract more cybersecurity talent.

Remote Work With Travel

I had a job that was remote, but I traveled for over 50% of the year. I don't know if you could call it "work from home" because I was never home.

I was traveling to sites to teach security compliance. In January, I traveled to Japan and Germany. Then, in February, I would be in Virginia and Hawaii. I was at each site for 4 – 5 days teaching. This doesn't sound too bad, but you have to factor in the travel days. Depending on the distance between locations, there might be 2 – 3 days of travel, 4 days if something goes wrong with the flight. At times, I would be away from home for about two weeks out of the month. On the days I was home, I would be preparing for my next class. It felt like I was gone all the time.

Aside from different remote work situations, there are also just bad work environments. I am not going to say any names, but I worked for one organization that made our lives a living hell. They would have us deliver a 50-page document and then have us redo it. They would call us into meetings and berate us in front of our peers. The client would go directly to our boss for minor issues and tell them we were incompetent. They would attack us on emails addressed to our supervisors, their bosses, and our coworkers.

It was a terrible situation where there was a lot of stress. There was an internal investigation where the organization found out that parts of the leaders among our clients didn't like the contract, so they were trying to sabotage it. It was so bad that congress got involved. As I said, it was bad.

We had flex workers, office workers, and people who worked 100% remote, and we all had a very bad time at that organization. Not all work from home situations are good.

If you find yourself in an environment that is toxic, working from home will not help you. It's best to just seek other employment.

Find a "Work from Home" Cybersecurity Job

These days most search engines and job sites have filters, categories, and other features that allow you to find a work from home job. You don't need to go to a specialized remote work site, although some of those are good.

The best method I have found for getting offered more work from home opportunities is to market my resume specifically for these positions. Using the simple methods I will describe, I have been able to get more technical recruiters and jobs contacting me for remote positions than I have applied for.

I do this in three steps:

- Remote Work Resume
- Upload to Multiple Job Sites
- Apply to Work From Home Jobs

We will go into greater detail on each of these, but you must know that these jobs are more competitive than normal jobs. More qualified people will be applying for these work from home positions. As a result, these jobs take longer to get.

In my experience, a normal job might take me three weeks to get from the time I apply to the time I get the offer letter. Work from home jobs take me longer to get on average. This may be because I am very picky and looking for higher pay positions.

I have found I need to be way faster in applying for jobs, and I need to apply for way more work from home jobs than the regular ones.

When you approach the work from home resume, you will need to add more keywords to attract more employers and technical recruiters. You will need to post your resume in twice as many places.

Remote Work Resume

The first thing we will do is create a simple application tracking system (ATS) compliant resume. This resume needs keywords relevant to the cybersecurity position you are trying to get into.

To get a free sample of an ATS-style cybersecurity resume, go to:

convocourses.com/courses/resume[1]

An ATS-style resume for cybersecurity looks like this:

Brian Noble

Phone number – email – City

Summary

Remote work preferred. 2 years of IT experience with a Public Trust security clearance. Skilled cybersecurity professional able to perform in a team and independently to get the jobs done. Well-versed in implementing NIST 800 and CIS-based security controls.

Education

Associate Degree – Information Technology – Fayetteville Community College – 2019

- Working on B.S. in C.S.
- Extensive training using digital spreadsheets and formulas efficiently

---

1. http://convocourses.com/courses/resume

- Earned a certificate in Security+ training

Certifications

CompTIA Security + Certification

Project Management Professional Certification (PMP)

Work Experience

Help Desk Support – TirePlanet – remote – April 2021–April 2022

- Troubleshooting end-users' laptops with network and software issues; supporting 150 users with multiple devices
- Managed Android and iPhone ensuring all company-owned mobile devices are tracked and data is encrypted
- Enabled audit logs on 34 mission-essential systems and 100 end-user laptops to conduct continuous monitoring and detect possible security incidents
- Created an incident response plan for all business essential servers supporting the southwest sites; virtual servers include Windows 2019 and RedHat systems

IT Customer Service – Ants – New Mexico – January 2020–December 2021

- Conducted quarterly risk assessment on over 200 business critical systems; created risk reports for the CIO and upper management
- Assisted the server team in installing 12 Windows 2019 servers, migrating legacy systems to a new operating system
- Provided remote technical support for the workstations of over 1,500 customers; patient with difficult customers

Skills

- Programming language: C+, HTML, Fortran, COBOL
- Security clearance: Secret, TS/SCI, Public Trust

The template is the easy part. What will take some work on your part is to get keywords into the resume. To find the correct keywords, you will need to research the market for the job you want.

For example, if you are trying to go into "cybersecurity investigations" or "cybersecurity analyst" work, you will need to start by conducting a search on that key phrase.

Use job sites and aggregators to search your key phrase of choice. You are looking for employers that have recently put out jobs for that key phrase.

Pay close attention to the job description requirements, skills, certifications, tools, and other things employers are looking for.

On LinkedIn, you can take this search deeper by looking into other people's resumes. Look for cybersecurity professionals in your field of choice and check out what keywords they have chosen.

You will want to use the same keywords, tools, and skills on your resume. I am not telling you to lie on your resume; I am telling you to look at your own skills, experience, and knowledge and use the same wording that the cybersecurity market is looking for.

For more on keywords and resume marketing, check out book 1, *Cybersecurity jobs Resume Marketing,* or check out the course at convocourses.com[2]

In this book, our main focus will be targeting cybersecurity work from home positions.

Work From Home Summary

For remote work in cybersecurity, we need to use the magic words: "Remote Work"

Well, actually, you have a few other magic words:

"Work from home"

"Hybrid"

"Telecommute"

You want to put this in your resume. In fact, you want to put them in the summary of your resume like this:

Summary

Work from home preferred. 3 years of cybersecurity, implementing security controls on business essential functions in accordance with security best practices detailed in CIS v8.

This summary has some keywords and starts off with our desire to "work from home." This is important because some technical recruiters and employers look for this.

I usually use the words "remote work preferred," but "work from home," "hybrid," and "telecommute" are more popular.

Experience Working Remotely

In 50% of the interviews I've had for "work from home" positions, they asked me if I have worked from home before. They ask this because not everyone does well in a work from home environment.

One of the first things you can do to indicate that you have worked remotely is to put it on top of your work experience, where you normally put the location of your previous employment. It will read like this:

IT Specialist

Oracle Labs, Remote; February 2020 to Current

Normally, the location of the business is put right up top just before the time frame that you worked there, but this is an opportunity to show that you worked remotely.

After listing the role, location, and timeframe, you can also mention that you worked from home like this:

- Updated security patches on 150 endpoint devices working from home, reducing the overall risks to the organization
- Wrote 4 enterprise-level cybersecurity policies and standards for a fortune 500 company coordinating with upper-level management while working from home

If you have never actually "worked from home," you have more than likely done lots of work remotely. Most organizations have systems that are at remote locations, and you can use this on your resume. If you have had any of the following situations, you have had exposure to remote work or remote work tools:

- Did the organization you work for allow VPNs?

- Did the employer allow flex work allowing people to work from home a few times a week?
- Did the business have sites at different locations?
- Did you ever have to do meetings over the phone?
- Were audio or video group calls ever done at the place you worked?
- Did you ever have to use Zoom, Teams, Skype, Webex, or any other video conferencing tools to coordinate with others to get work done?
- Did you have calls with clients and customers to help them with a technical service?

If you have worked in any of these situations, there may be something you can put on your resume about working remotely or working with tools for working remotely. Let me explain how you can mention this in your work experience.

- Serviced 164 endpoint devices for remote work employees by updating security patches and antivirus signatures on them; improved the resilience of the organization's business function
- Subject matter expert on regular remote configuration management meetings that included major Windows Server 2019 migration; meetings completed via Zoom and Teams collaborations

In these two examples, we managed to squeeze in the keyword "remote." We also explain that we have been successful in doing remote work. In the example, we mention the latest and greatest video conferencing tools.

While we can work well in a team collaborating remotely, we want to mention that we can work independently with little or no instruction.

- Self-directed on large and small cybersecurity projects, such as

the configuration of VPN on 67 mobile devices
- Initiated risk reduction tasks, including the creation of cybersecurity reports on the top 20 vulnerabilities within the organization

Employers want to know that you can work independently with no one constantly holding your hand. If you land a work from home job, you will need to be able to get the job done with little or no supervision. So we want to put this in the resume.

You will also notice that I use numbers in the sample resume text. This is done to show the impact of cybersecurity actions.

To get a free sample of an ATS-style cybersecurity resume, go to:

convocourses.com/courses/resume[1]

---

1. http://convocourses.com/courses/resume

Market Your WFH Resume

Once you have a solid resume stating your preference for a work from home job and your ability to work remotely, it's time to publish this resume on the job sites.

Find the Top 10 Job Sites

Search for the top job sites in your country. You can do this by going to your favorite search engine and typing the key phrase:

- Top Job Sites in the USA
- Top Job Sites in Canada
- Top Job Sites in the U.K.
- Top Job Sites in Kenya

Use whatever country you are trying to get work in. Since this is a work from home job, it can be any country. But just know that each country has its own challenges, laws, and restrictions.

Some countries don't have many remote jobs because they don't have the infrastructure or culture to allow work from home. Sometimes "work from home" is just not a thing there.

Many cybersecurity jobs in the USA restrict foreign nationals from working with sensitive data. There are jobs that hire foreign nationals, but you just have to look for them.

Some companies allow remote work, but only if you work remotely from their country.

Finding work from home jobs that will fit your situation is going to be hard, so you will need to find at least ten of the top job sites to post your resume.

If you are really serious, find 20 or 30 sites in more than one country.

Create a Profile Post Your Resume

WARNING:

We interrupt this book for a warning about how effective this is! *This really works! Once I did this, I started getting contacted by dozens of technical recruiters and employers per week. I strongly suggest you use a throw-away email and a different phone number. This is so effective that I get contacts throughout the day at inconvenient times.*

You must use a different email, not post your full address, and must use a different phone number. This is not a joke.

This part of the process will take the longest time, especially if you are posting on ten sites. A solid ATS-style resume will make your work here easier because many sites just allow you to upload your resume, and 50% of the work is done.

The most effective job sites will have a detailed profile for you to fill out. You will need to take time to properly complete this because the site will use this profile to find you. The site's algorithm will use the data in the profile and your uploaded resume to match you with jobs.

So, when the profile has a section to fill out your skills, you must put in all your cybersecurity skills. For a deeper dive into some suggested career paths and associated skills, check out *Book 2: Cybersecurity Jobs and Career Paths.* You can also use other people's resumes posted on sites like LinkedIn.

The only parts of the profile you will skip are the ones that are not relevant.

For example, I don't know any other languages, so I have to skip the language section. But if you know more than one language, that's a big deal, and you need to put that on your profile.

The profile is very important for work from home cybersecurity jobs because most employers and technical recruiters are looking at the top 10 job sites. If your profile doesn't list a valuable skill, certification, or experience that they are looking for, they will find someone else. And if you don't even have a profile, they will not find you at all.

The more time you put into filling out these profiles, the better your chances because it will increase your probability of being found.

For a deeper dive into resume marketing, check out *Book 1: Cybersecurity Jobs Resume Marketing.*

Apply for Remote Jobs

To get a good work from home job, it's not enough to have a good resume and post it on ten job sites. The next step is also important. You need to apply for as many remote jobs as possible.

Once your perfect, ATS-style cybersecurity resume is posted on NO less than ten of the top job sites, you need to conduct a search for jobs on that site.

The great thing about posting on these job sites and filling out a complete profile is that the site will do most of the work for you. As I said, the algorithm will actively find jobs that match you.

But with work from home jobs, there is one more step we need to take to find these jobs.

We need to filter for remote positions. For example, if we're looking for an "IT customer support" job, we want to filter for "remote work."

Most of the top job sites have a filter called "remote work" or "work from home."

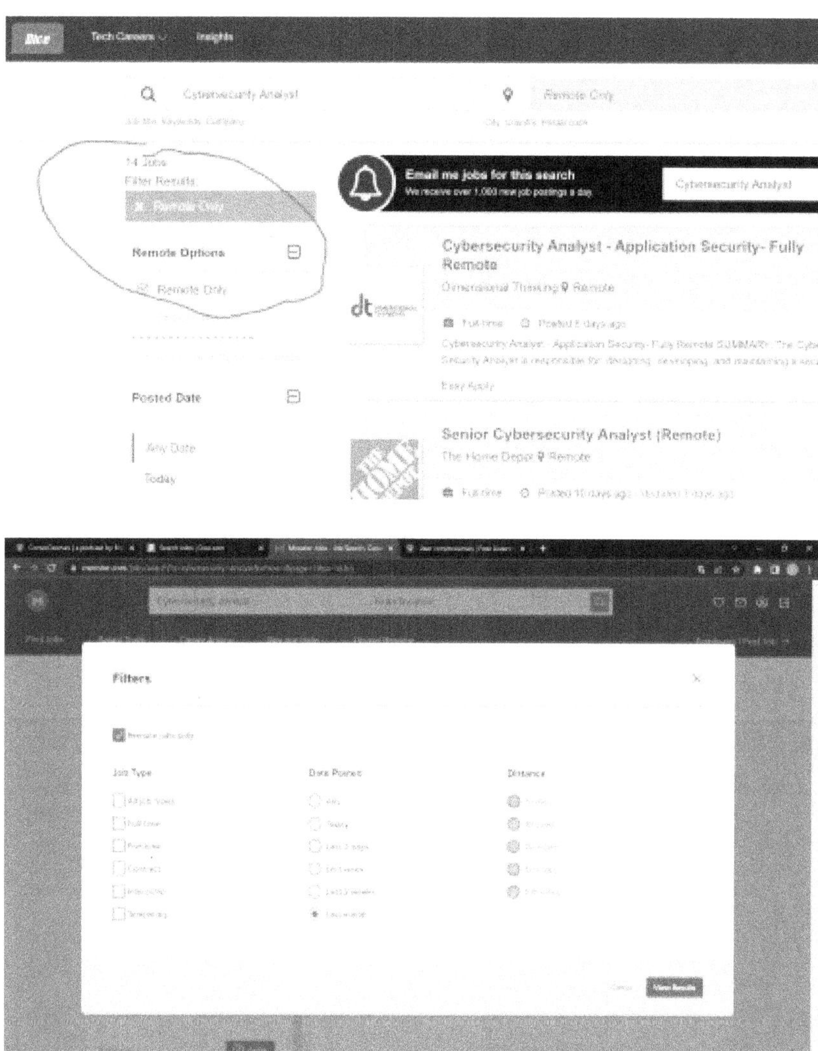

For example, the job search site Dice.com has a "Remote Only" check box. Monster.com and others also have this feature.

Another thing you want to add to the filter is a time frame of when the jobs were posted.

The default time frame of posting on some job sites is "Any." This means that the search results come from positions that were posted three months ago or longer. After 30 days, work from home jobs are usually long gone (especially if they are good or pay well).

You need to use this filter and look for jobs that have been posted in the last 30 days or sooner; work from home jobs are taken fast.

Remote work is much more competitive than the regular local jobs out there. You will need to apply for as many remote, flex, telecommute, and 100% work from home jobs as possible.

We want to do this on multiple sites. I cannot stress this enough. Three of four top sites will not be enough to get a remote job. You need to apply for dozens of jobs on ten or more job sites.

The search engines, Google.com, Bing, and others also have job search features. They are usually just pulling data from all over the Internet to show you results, but all you have to do is type in "Cybersecurity Jobs." Really, anything searched with "Jobs" in the key phrase will have the search engines job aggregator pop up.

Top Cyber security jobs | Increase Your Salary 10-20%

Apply for Jobs on Monster.com | Jobs In Colorado Springs

Jobs Near You (Hiring Now) | Job Search — Jobs Hiring Now

Cyber Security Job Hiring | $15-57/Hr (No Experience Req.)

3 urgent Openings | Hiring Immediately | Cyber Security Jobs

Sr Staff Cybersecurity Engineer
Northrop Grumman
Colorado Springs, CO · Full-time

Use Alerts & Notifications

Most job sites have a feature that will notify you when a job matches what you are looking for. As soon as the employer posts the job, the site will send you a text or email. This feature is called "Alerts" or "Notifications."

With work from home jobs, this is something you may want to use because these jobs go very fast.

How you set up the alert depends on the job site aggregator. With Google jobs, Linkedin, and Dice.com, you conduct a search for the cybersecurity job you are looking for. So you would do your normal job search, such as "cybersecurity analyst." If you are having a hard time finding a position, make sure it is a broad term such as "cybersecurity" filter for "remote work only," and you can set up the alert after the search.

Google
cybersecurity jobs
Jobs
Saved
Work from home
Did you mean: cyber security jobs
Cyber Security Engineer
AMS Staffing Inc.
Cybersecurity Analyst - Application Security- Fully Remote
Dimensional Thinking
Cybersecurity Incident Response Analyst (Remote)
ID.me
Alerts are on for this search
Cyber Security Engineer
AMS Staffing Inc
Apply on Dice
Please send your resume in WORD format should you be interest
Must live in the United States*
Job Title: Cyber Security Engineer
Location: 100% Remote
Term: Full time
3rd Party C2C/Transfer: No
Please reply with an updated resume in Microsoft Word format

Jobs
Cybersecurity Systems Analyst Senior with Security Clearance
Apply
Save

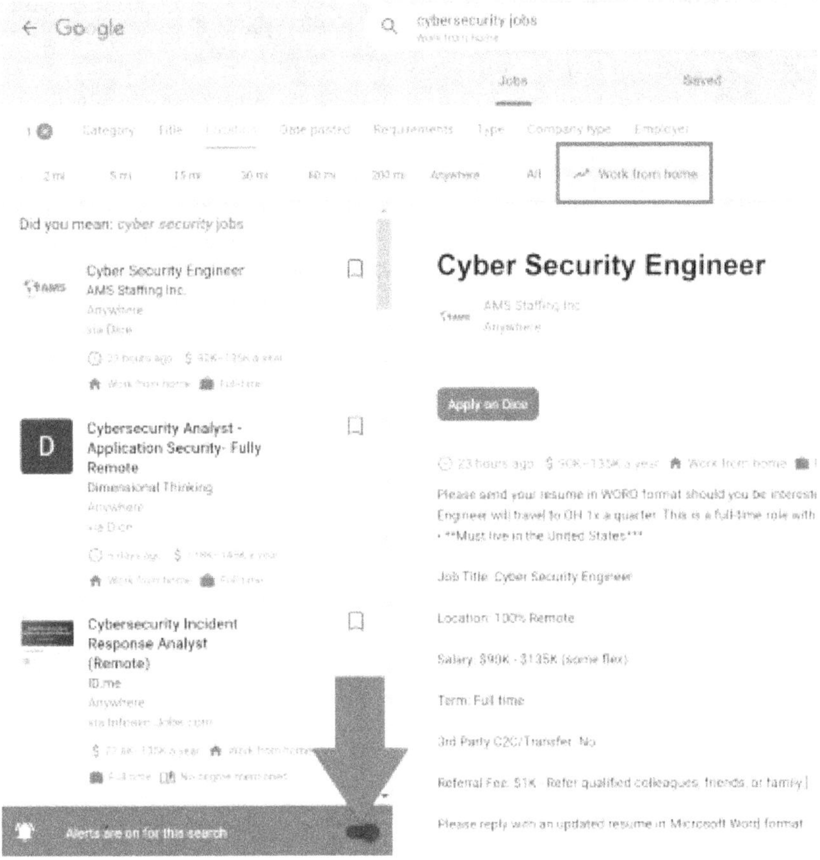

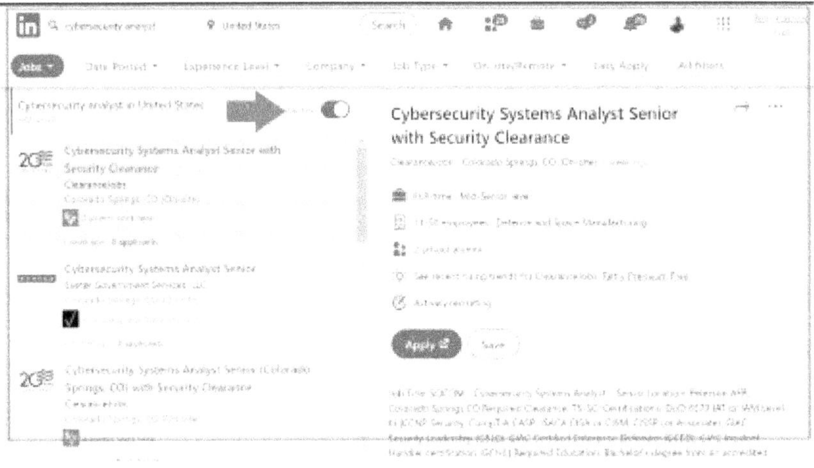

On Monster, the search is set up in a separate part of the site. Just be aware that you may need to hunt for this feature.

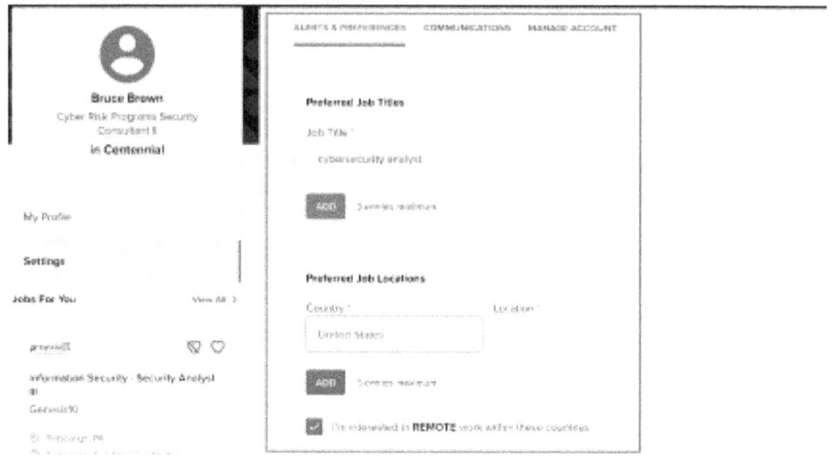

Be Open Minded

What I have had to do in finding remote positions is be open to different roles. There was a time when I ONLY wanted remote security information event manager (SIEM) jobs. It was because a former coworker told me that he had been working as a SIEM engineer from home, making about 200k. Another friend of mine was a Unix administrator working from home. These were both hands-on technical jobs.

I thought these were the only jobs available for remote work. I thought it had to be highly technical and from a very large company because anyone I knew who landed these rare remote jobs had this exact situation. I wanted this so bad that I got fixated on this one thing.

I was wrong.

I have had cybersecurity teaching jobs, policy writing jobs, and information system security jobs that were remote. I have been offered opportunities to do program management, system engineering, and a huge variety of jobs that were 100% remote.

You need to have an open mind for remote work because there are all kinds of situations and positions that need your help.

My first work from home position came from a blog post I did. I was writing a blog that broke down how to do security compliance for the government, and an employer found it.

She had a small business that had a 400,000-dollar contract with the military. She had so much work that she could no longer do it all herself. She reached out to me and offered me a job helping her teach.

That was also the first time I grossed 100,000 dollars for the year.

Avoid Scams

You have to be open minded, but you have to avoid scams.

In your search for remote jobs, you will definitely run into scams. I just want to warn you about this. There are a lot of scammers online offering remote positions. These people are trying to get you to give them your personally identifiable information and money or trying to exploit you in some way for their own gain.

Here are signs that let you know that you are probably dealing with a scam:

- If it sounds too good to be true, then it probably is
- If they are asking for personal information such as your social security number
- They want you to send them money before you have access to the employer
- The job has nothing to do with your profession
- They are offering a once-in-a-lifetime business opportunity
- They want you to download something or click a link before you can even have a screening interview.

I don't want to scare you from a great potential remote cybersecurity job. I just want you to proceed with caution and take time to research the potential employer.

There are some amazing opportunities that I have been offered. More than once, the owner of a small company called me, gave me a 20-minute Interview, and offered me a position immediately. It turned out to be real. They didn't ask me for my social or ask me to pay some fee before I got the job. In each case, the small business ended up giving me information that put them at risk because if I knew about the client and the contract, I could potentially solicit their customer directly. I knew it was real because I was able to verify the organization myself with the information they gave me about the work.

My point is whenever this happens, I am very suspicious! And you should be too. Don't jump into anything too fast. Remember, you are interviewing the employer as much as they are interviewing you. You need to do your due diligence. You need to research the organization. Check them out online. What is their reputation? Can you find others who have worked for them? Can you verify their real contact information? Are they putting themselves at risk just by telling you about the opportunity? For example, after a non-disclosure agreement, are they giving you sensitive information that could put their business at risk?

Work from home interview

With work from home jobs, it all comes down to the interview. This is sometimes the first and last time they will see your face, so you have to make it count.

More than normal office jobs, an online interview is pivotal for remote work. The resume just gets your foot in the door.

One of the things that you have to absolutely make sure is good is your internet connection and your online presentation:

- Your audio and visual during the interview has to be solid
- Make sure you are dressed in business casual
- Be online and ready before the interview starts

The interview process for cybersecurity usually consists of an average of three separate contacts before an actual job is offered. In my many interviews this process usually consists of the following:

- The screener contact
- Hiring manager/H.R. department Interview
- Manager/Technical Interview

The Screener

With cybersecurity jobs, you will usually have a screener contact you. This is a technical recruiter consisting of a call, an email, or both. They don't usually know much about IT or the actual job you will do. You are probably the fifty-seventh person they have emailed, called, or messaged for this position. This call will be short. They only want to know if you are interested in the position, if you are qualified, and if you are available. Sometimes, they will have you do a non-disclosure agreement if it is a staffing agency; this is a common practice. You don't need to give them any personal information at this point. There is no commitment to anything yet. I don't normally sign an NDA until I am sure I am qualified and want to know more about the opportunity. If I am interested, I start by reading the job description and requirements.

They may ask if you are willing to travel. Sometimes they will let you know about the salary range. If you match the job requirements and are interested, the screener will contact someone closer to the project. This will be the human resources department, a hiring manager, or even someone from the team you would be working with.

Hiring Manager and H.R. Department

If the organization's process is thorough, the screener will send your contact information and resume to an office that will conduct further screening. This will be the employer's hiring manager or Human Resources department. In my experience, this is a stress-free 15 to 20-minute introduction to the company over the phone.

They take a quick look at your resume. They ask more questions to see if you fit into the role. It is usually just an informal, informative session where they tell you about the company and the role that they are filling. Questions they ask include things like:

- Have you worked remotely before?
- Where are you currently working?
- Have you ever heard of our company before?
- Are you willing to travel (if applicable)?
- Are you willing to relocate (if applicable)?

They might ask very generic questions about your experience working with a certain aspect of cybersecurity or using a certain tool. For example, they might say something like:

"Can you tell me about your cybersecurity experience?"

Or

"Have you ever worked with the Department of Defense before?"

They explain the benefits, mention the salary, the hiring process, and other general information about working with the client and the company. At this point, they try to sell you on the idea of working for the company if they think you might be a good fit. There are no details about the tasks of the job because H.R. will not know much about it. Any questions you have will have to be about your work as an employee working for this employer.

On some occasions, the hiring managers tried to talk me into working locally or even relocating. Sometimes, it's just not a good fit, and we politely end the Interviewing process.

But if everything is good, the hiring manager or human resources office will set you up on a meeting with the technical team or the managers directly involved with the job. When this happens, I get a formal email inviting me to a video conference call.

Technical and Management Interview

In my last few interviews for remote jobs, the employer used the top enterprise-level video conferencing software. At the time of this writing, it has been Microsoft Teams, Zoom, Skype, or Webex.

Make sure you test the video conferencing software to make sure it works before the call.

You will be expected to turn on your video. What I do is download the applicable software and test the video and audio on the system I will be using. You may need to create an account on the application they are using.

I ensure the lighting is good and I am in a quiet room. If possible, record yourself with the software and watch yourself perform a mock interview.

Before the video, do the following:

- Review the job description and see how it matches your own experience
- Review your own resume
- Check the sound, lighting, and video using the software they selected
- Practice a mock interview
- Dress business casual
- Remove all background distractions

What you don't want to do is:

- Set everything up 5 minutes before the interview
- Have technical difficulties 10 minutes into the call
- Be smoking or eating chips during the interview
- Chewing gum during the interview

- Pretend like you know everything
- Wear pajamas with kids running around in the background

Instead, be on the call ready to go 15 minutes before the call. I have found 15 minutes is best because there are often technical difficulties that take a few minutes to fix. You need to be the best-dressed person on the call. While everybody else is dressed in their T-shirts and baseball caps, you will be in button-down business casual with the best mic and camera and be the most prepared person on the call.

If you take the time to dive deep into their job description and what they require, you will have a solid understanding of what kinds of questions they will ask.

During the interview, they will say things like:

"I can see on your resume that you have experience setting up audit logs on Linux. Can you tell me more about that?"

OR

"The team really needs someone who knows how to implement patches on Windows and do vulnerability management. Do you have experience doing that?"

Open-ended questions are an opportunity to tell them about your experience. You need to look directly into the camera and answer just like you practiced.

There's a habit that we have of looking at ourselves when talking on video. We look at ourselves on the video screen while speaking, but when we do this, our eyes are not looking at the people we are talking to. You need to look into the lens of the camera and speak toward the mic. Practice doing this, record yourself doing it, and play it back.

The types of questions will be based on the requirements in the job description.

At the end of the interview, they will ask you if you have any questions for them. I usually ask questions to identify any red flags like overworked employees and travel. Here are some examples of questions that I ask:

- Is there any shift work?
- What are the typical work hours?
- Is there overtime?
- Who is the client?
- How much travel is there?
- Is there a high turnover rate?
- What are the biggest challenges of the position?
- How many systems will I manage?
- What are some pros and cons about the job?
- How much time off do we get per year?

Company Research

As much as they are interviewing you, you need to interview them. Look into what the company does, its objectives, its core values, and who they serve. You need to look into the following:

- How many sites do they have, and where are they located?
- Look at all the sites that they have all around the world.
- What is the organization's gross revenue?
- What are the salaries of average employees?
- Are employees posting negative comments are videos about them?
- Have they recently had a breach?

You might be able to find the average salary or even the position you are going for on sites like Payscale, Salary.com, or Glassdoor.

Go to social media to see if you can find former employees talking about the company.

You need to know exactly what you are getting into with the company.

One thing I want to repeat is to read through the job description, requirements, and preferences. Preferences will sometimes tell you a lot about what tools they use.

Two Remote Jobs

With remote work, I have had the opportunity to work two high-paying jobs at once. When you are not in an office, commuting to an office, or having coworkers chat you up about things that have little or nothing to do with your job, it's amazing how much extra time you have between creating reports, vulnerabilities to analyze, or meaningless impromptu meetings on the plan of action and milestones.

If you are considering doing this, make sure you don't have a conflict of interest with soulless litigious powerhouses like governments or financial institutions. For example, you should not work for two competing organizations in the same industry. Another example is working as an auditor and working for the organization that will be audited.

These types of shenanigans can win you a free lunch in federal prison or, at the very least, get you paying for a lawyer's hair transplant surgery. Hair transplants are not cheap, buddy. Trust me... I know.

Another thing to avoid is violating your contract. Some contracts explicitly tell you not to work for other organizations during work hours.

You might be thinking, "Bruce, I've been doing this for a while. I have not been caught."

Ok. If you want to be picking up soap in jail, be my guest. Listen, it's not illegal to do this (if you do it right). I am just saying to proceed with caution and at your own risk.

In cybersecurity, you will be offered many positions that you can do remotely, and it occurs to you that you can do more than one.

I have done it a few times. There is a right way and a wrong way to have two jobs.

I have done the following:

- Quick Temporary Side Jobs
- Secondary Part-time Cybersecurity Job
- Two Full-time jobs

Quick temporary side jobs

What I do from time to time is temporary cybersecurity work that consists of doing one task that will only take a few weeks or less to do. For example, it might be creating a system security plan or running a scan. This type of work is not dependent on my working in a shift or from 8 am to 4 pm because the focus is just to get the work done in a certain period. We just agree on what the work will be, how long it will take, and how much it will cost. This is usually an hourly rate, but I have written documents or created training for an organization for a flat fee.

These types of jobs are usually very small businesses that don't need anyone to do the work full-time because it is a one-time thing.

Secondary Part-time Cybersecurity Job

This is work where they don't need someone working 8 hours every day. But they need someone to fill a role with multiple tasks, talk to the clients, and join meetings.

This is doable, but I have had success with this only if I tell that part-time job that I have a full-time job. I have to let them know that my full-time job takes priority. This is important because there are occasions when your full-time position will overlap with the part-time job and you have to make sure this does not happen.

Two Full-Time Jobs

DO NOT DO THIS!

There are only 24 hours in a day. If you are working 16 hours a day, at weekends, and on holidays, you will burn out fast.

Psychologically, you will start to question the meaning of life. You start to think to yourself, "Am I only alive to work? How much money do I need?"

You will begin to have hallucinations, and you will go bald as you slowly descend into madness!

Ok, I am exaggerating, but I am telling you this is just not healthy. If you do decide to work two full-time jobs like an idiot, make sure you only do it for a limited amount of time because the stress of doing this in a cybersecurity position is very high.

It's your life, and you can do whatever you want. But if you have landed a really good full-time, cybersecurity position, 100% remote job with good pay and good benefits, take time to realize the risk you run by violating that organization's trust.

I have done it before, and I do not recommend it. Beyond risking the "trust of a company," it gets into working yourself to burn out. It's not fun.

Doing this pays like crazy. But remember this:

- Pigs get fat. Hogs get slaughtered.

You Can Do it

The last thing I want to say about getting a work from home job is that you can do it. There's a gold rush for these work from home positions in cybersecurity. As soon as they're posted, the best and brightest are going after these jobs. Competition is much more fierce with work from home positions.

Don't be discouraged. If you use the techniques in this book, you will get lots of opportunities for remote work.

www.ingramcontent.com/pod-product-compliance
Lightning Source LLC
Chambersburg PA
CBHW052237150726
48002CB00003B/1477